www.finishinglinepress.com

Climbing the Fire Escape, Flipping the Raft

Poems on Women in Movies

poems by

Kathleen McClung

Finishing Line Press
Georgetown, Kentucky

Climbing the Fire Escape, Flipping the Raft

Poems on Women in Movies

ACKNOWLEDGMENTS

Thank you to the editors of these literary journals and anthologies that first
published the following poems:

All the Women Came & Sang: A Poetry Collection of Women's Voices: "The
Power of the Dog Villanelle," "TransSiberian Sonnet"
Mezzo Cammin: "Thelma and Louise Alternate Ending," "Dangerous
Liaisons Triolet"
Persimmon Tree: "The Wizard of Oz Abecedarian"
Unsinkable: Poetry Inspired by the Titanic: "Watching 'Titanic' on Retreat at
Tomales Bay"

"Watching 'Titanic' on Retreat at Tomales Bay" won the Grand Prize in the
Ina Coolbrith Circle's 2022 102nd Annual Contest
 "Thelma and Louise Alternate Ending" and "Wind River Villanelle" received
Honorable Mentions in the Ina Coolbrith Circle's 2023 96th Annual Poets'
Dinner Contest.
"The Walk" Sonnet won Third Place in the Helen Schaible 2023 International
Sonnet Contest and was shortlisted for the 2025 Kim Bridgford Memorial
Sonnet Contest.

Publisher: Leah Huete de Maines
Editor: Christen Kincaid
Cover Art: Nancy Buffum
Author Photo: Tom McAninley
Cover Design: Elizabeth Maines McCleavy

Order online: www.finishinglinepress.com
also available on amazon.com

Author inquiries and mail orders:
Finishing Line Press
PO Box 1626
Georgetown, Kentucky 40324
USA

Contents

Introduction ix

"The Power of the Dog" Villanelle 1

"Wind River" Villanelle 2

"Fences" Sonnet 3

"The Walk" Sonnet 4

"TransSiberian" Sonnet 5

"Panic Room" Pantoum 6

"Blow" Abecedarian 7

"Limbo" Triolet 8

"The Wings of the Dove" Double Sonnet 9

Watching "Titanic" on Retreat at Tomales Bay 10

"Fargo" Pantoum 12

"Thelma and Louise" Alternate Ending 14

"The Grifters" Sestina 15

"The River Wild" Mirror Sonnet 17

"Where Angels Fear to Tread" Triolet 18

"Dangerous Liaisons" Triolet 19

"Rear Window" Pantoum 20

"The Wizard of Oz" Abecedarian 22

Appendix: The Movie Makers 23

Introduction

The summer I turned eighteen I worked at the Aladdin Theater on East Colfax Avenue in Denver, Colorado. Some shifts I sold tickets inside the glassed-in booth. Other shifts I worked behind the candy counter in the lobby. I much preferred the simplicity of exchanging tickets for cold, hard cash. In 1978 there were no credit card swipers in that booth, let alone Square, PayPal, Venmo, Zelle. People slid a five or a ten beneath the glass. Sometimes a twenty. I slid back a small, printed rectangle. Done deal.

At the end of my shift, I often grabbed a seat in the back of the cavernous theater to watch whatever movie happened to be projected onto the screen. Yes, I watched a lot of made-for-TV movies at home, and my parents took my sister and me to drive-in movies in the summer when we were kids, but this viewing was different. Better. All mine. My eighteen-year-old body sat in an itchy, fold-down chair inside the Aladdin Theater, but my imagination traveled far away, far from East Colfax Avenue.

Fast forward forty plus years to the Covid-19 pandemic of 2020 and the shut-down of much of the world—schools, libraries, churches, restaurants, theaters, department stores, playgrounds, campgrounds. We stayed home. Millions of us. For months. Yes, yes, I read. I'm a teacher. I read words on computer screens large and small, words in books, words in magazines and journals and, yes, print newspapers. I Zoomed. I walked. I could have decluttered my apartment, brought order and tidiness and dust-free shelves. But no. Instead, when I wasn't reading, I watched movies. A LOT of movies. Some terrific. Some dreadful. Most, though, somewhere in between. In all of them, I paid close attention to the women characters—the brave and daring ones, of course, the ones who battled monsters, looked for clues in dresser drawers, interrupted bad guys feeding other bad guys into wood chippers. But also the quiet women, the hemmed-in-by-circumstances women. Entering their worlds for two hours at a time—and then staying in their worlds to write poems—helped lift me out of pandemic isolation in the way those summer days inside the darkened Aladdin Theater helped inspire, intrigue and console my eighteen-year-old self.

This collection consists of eighteen of these poems on women in movies. I wrote them all between 2020-2023 and dedicate each poem to the actress whose performance lingered in my mind. I've included an Appendix listing these eighteen films, along with their dates, directors, and screenwriters. I encourage you to watch them. The formal poems here—sonnets, pantoums, villanelles, triolets, sestinas, abecedarians, and syllabics—grew out of my lifelong love of movies and my need to dwell, if only for a little while, in other worlds not suffering from a pandemic. I am grateful to the women and men who collaborated in earlier times to create these worlds.

May we continue all kinds of creative collaborations of our own.

"The Power of the Dog" Villanelle
for Kirsten Dunst

She tutors him. He's stiff and ill at ease.
Montana sky's both bridesmaid and best man
for Rose and George. The only melody's

a wisp of wind that lifts her lace, a breeze
through grass encircling dirt road, one lane.
She tutors him. He's stiff and ill at ease.

Perhaps he's never danced. Festivities
so rare for ranchers' sons. Such dry terrain
for Rose and George. His brother's cruelties

will savage her in days ahead. Whiskeys
will cloud her mind, provide no healing rain,
no tutoring. Rose, stiff and ill at ease,

will fade until her son Peter crafts strategies
that silence her tormentor, Phil, and end the pain
for Rose and George's fragile family.

A brother dies. The poison—secrecies.
A marriage slowly mends. They dance again.
Truth tutors them. Once stiff and ill at ease,
both Rose and George embrace some solace, peace.

"Wind River" Villanelle
for Elizabeth Olsen

You look for clues. So much you don't yet know
although the FBI has trained you well.
She ran barefoot across Wyoming snow,

a daughter, sister, friend, 18. Follow
advice from wolf hunters, from owls, to help
you look for clues. So much you don't yet know

about this frozen land, twenty below,
about this reservation. You can tell
she ran barefoot across Wyoming snow

but not why yet, not where she tried to go
or what she fled that night before she fell.
You gather clues. So much you don't yet know

about her death, the forces long ago
that hardened inside men like stone or shell
or barren ground beneath Wyoming snow.

Oil workers, whiskey, rape. Your search will show
her bruises. Fists, like wind—perennial.
You look for truth. So much you don't yet know.
She ran barefoot across Wyoming snow.

"Fences" Sonnet
for Viola Davis

You play the numbers, Rose, a nickel here,
a nickel there. Oh, Troy does not agree—
just money thrown away, the raconteur
declares. Your food shopping—the A & P,
but Troy pays ten cents more, with gratitude,
at Bella's *where I'm treated right.* Your man
fills up the whole house, Rose, your voice subdued,
your son afraid. You listen to Troy's plans,
his tales of baseball, wrestling Death, a song
about an old dog, Blue. And you embrace
and raise the child from Troy's affair. How strong
your compass, Rose, how steadily you face
each Pittsburgh sunrise over this wood fence.
Forgiveness, your own form of eloquence.

"The Walk" Sonnet
for Charlotte Le Bon

He walks the wire at dawn, a speck between
Twin Towers not yet occupied. And you,
Annie, his muse, keep watch all night, ravine
of concrete, not of grass. He's planned, pursued
this dream six years, accomplices all men
except for you, faithful below his wire.
Phillipe once stole your busking audience—
your folk guitar no match for juggling fire.
A charming unicyclist—brash, bold,
a mime's blithe arrogance. He will not wear
a safety line. He will not be controlled
or harnessed. Now he breathes the morning air,
prepares to take a step. You drink a cup
of coffee, crane your neck, look up   up   up.

"TransSiberian" Sonnet
for Emily Mortimer

Erase your photographs, Jessie. No trace
of Carlos smiling, no hawks across the sky,
no ceiling of a ruined church, no face
of a forgotten saint. Detectives try
a soft approach at first. Do not be lured
by gentle wit, Grinko's small talk inside
the train. He calculates each charming word.
Delete, discard what he might see, and hide
regret in nesting dolls as Carlos hid
the heroin before he died, fence post
a weapon in your hands. Jessie, get rid
of everything, all record of what's lost.
Trust only snowdrifts near the house of prayer—
custodians of secrets, bitter air.

"Panic Room" Pantoum
for Jodie Foster

Meg Altman is divorcing a pharmaceutical executive.
Her daughter is ten and diabetic. Droll in a Sid Vicious t-shirt.
First night in the huge new house, Upper West Side—
rain, pizza, Coke, and too much red wine for Meg.

Her daughter is ten and diabetic. Droll in a Sid Vicious t-shirt,
afraid of the dark. Meg leaves the bedroom door open.
Rain, pizza, Coke, and too much red wine for Meg,
splitting headache, insomnia, a discovery on the surveillance camera—

unafraid of the dark, ski-masked men jimmy a basement door open.
The rest of the movie mother and daughter fight to survive inside the house
way past headaches, insomnia, and discoveries on the surveillance cameras.
Among the three men, secrets unfold and double crossings. One gets shot.

The rest of the movie mother and daughter fight to survive inside the house,
not unlike many women living in real-life houses—tract homes and bungalows.
Among lots of men, secrets unfold and double crossings. Some get shot.
Meg and her daughter, however, hide out in a locked panic room.

Most women living in real-life houses—tract homes and bungalows—
do not have any high-tech safe space, a bonus room like a bank vault.
Meg and her daughter, however, come out of the locked panic room.
Surveillance cameras get smashed. (More violence I fast-forward through.)

I do not have a high-tech safe space, no bonus room like a bank vault,
but I know how the movie ends. The women survive. They downsize
after surveillance cameras get smashed & more violence I fast-forward through.
Note to self: avoid marrying or divorcing a pharmaceutical executive.

"Blow" Abecedarian
for Penelope Cruz

At Diego's wedding in Colombia, the two of you
begin, each asking, "Why are you smiling?" Your
cigarette—a flogging stick—and your red
dress, the burning end, the flame.
Everyone knows nothing good will come, except
for the baby you make with George. But even this
girl will turn on him eventually—so much like
his mother, so much like you, Mirtha.
Intimacy cracks in a thousand ways. Cocaine
just sprays glitter on brokenness to
keep it shiny for a while. George does
leave the business, jumps bail, gets clean, but his
money—all of it—vanishes from the Panamanian bank.
Now the final break, the very last specks
of the glitter. You snort coke in the car. A cop
pulls over the convertible—George
quiet at the wheel, you skeletal and
raging in a red hanky of a dress,
screaming words like *faggot & fugitive*, half-
truths these curses flung into the night air, not
unlike his mother's words in Massachusetts.
Vindication eludes both you and her. Now the only
weapon left to wield—a bitter potion of banishment &
excision, a permanent turning of
your backs on a husband, on a son, once loved, now a
zero, a nothing, a never was.

"Limbo" Triolet
for Mary Elizabeth Mastrantonio

You sang torch songs in clubs. Your daughter writes
elusive tales of frontier families
who strive but fail to outlast cold, wet nights.
You sang torch songs in clubs. Your daughter writes.
You're stranded, warmed by feeble firelight,
the branches snapped from island hemlock trees.
You sang torch songs. Not now. Your daughter writes
elusive tales of frontier families.

"The Wings of the Dove" Double Sonnet
for Helena Bonham-Carter

Kate Croy, your mother's dead. Your father drinks,
takes opium, ten shillings every week
Aunt Maude pays him to stay away. She thinks
it prudent that he dwell elsewhere, not speak
with you at all. She wants the best for you,
of course. In 1910, this means huge hats
and stodgy suitors, titled, well-to-do.
Your lover Merton is forbidden too, his flat
off-limits. No more rendezvous. (He writes,
and London journalists rank down below
eaters of opium.)   Your Boston friend invites
Merton and you to Venice, and you go,
of course, exuberant—a change of scene
away from Maude, from rain and from routine—

but mainly Venice offers you long hours
of pleasure, freedom. You concoct a plan
while ambling through museums, climbing towers
the three of you—the rich American
who's deathly ill, the journalist, and you.
You pair them up: Milly, Merton. You hope
she'll leave him money in her will, free up the two
of you to flee Aunt Maude at last, elope.
But Henry James has spun this knotted tale.
Your jealousy, your flaw. Soon Milly dies, aware
and yet forgiving of your scheme. You fail
to own his heart in full. He cannot swear
he doesn't love her ghost, her guileless grace.
Deceit ends, Kate. But sorrow takes its place.

Watching "Titanic" on Retreat at Tomales Bay
for Kate Winslet

I know how this ends.
Jack freezes. Rose lives.
It's 1 a.m. I'm
muting the remote,
afraid the screaming
will wake the people
next door. Who am I
to mess with a good
night's sleep for strangers?

I know how this ends.
Rose blows a whistle.
It's feeble at first.
They almost miss her,
the rescuers, row
past bobbing corpses
in life preservers.
But Rose blasts away
in the dark ocean.

I know how this ends.
Rose hides in a cloak,
eludes the horrid
fiancé who'd chased
her with a gun but
kept missing each shot.
They marry others.
Rose gets very old,
becomes a potter.

I know how this ends.
There's a twist with the
diamond. I click OFF,
though. It's crazy late.
I'm sick of the ads

for online weight loss,
Befores and Afters
supposedly proof.
I drift off by three.

"Fargo" Pantoum
for Frances McDormand

Marge Gunderson, a pregnant police chief, wakes up early.
Winter. Brainerd, Minnesota. Three dead bodies.
She vomits at the crime scene—morning sickness,
not revulsion. Marge is sensible, matter-of-fact.

Winter. Brainerd, Minnesota. Three dead bodies—
shot at close range. Marge leads with logic,
not revulsion. She is sensible, matter-of-fact,
measures footprints in snow, applies inductive reasoning

to shootings at close range. Marge leads with logic,
demurs politely with a colleague's erroneous conclusion,
measures footprints in snow, applies inductive reasoning,
astutely interviews two young truck stop prostitutes.

Marge demurs politely with a colleague's erroneous conclusion,
travels to Minneapolis following up on leads
from astutely interviewing two young truck stop prostitutes.
She agrees to meet an old high school classmate in the hotel bar

when she travels to Minneapolis following up on leads.
Mike Yanagita is supposedly a lonely widower.
Marge meets her old high school classmate in the hotel bar,
listens, sips through a straw, doubt blooming on her face.

Mike Yanagita is not, in fact, a lonely widower.
He lies. So does Jerry Lundegaard. Marge visits his car dealership,
listens, sips through his evasions, doubt blooming on her face.
Lundegaard hired two kidnappers. He has an elaborate ransom scheme.

Lundegaard lies. He's deep in debt. Marge visits his car dealership.
The kidnappers kill his wife, father-in-law, and a parking attendant.
Lundegaard hired two kidnappers. He has an elaborate ransom scheme,
but the taciturn one kills the chatty one, stuffs him in a wood chipper.

The kidnappers kill the wife, father-in-law, and a parking attendant.
Driving to Brainerd, Marge discovers their hideout near Moose Lake.
The taciturn one kills the chatty one, stuffs him in a woodchipper.
Marge draws her gun, yells "Police!" (The woodchipper's very loud.)

Driving to Brainerd, Marge discovers their hideout near Moose Lake,
eventually handcuffs the kidnapper but has to shoot him in the leg
after she draws her gun, yells "Police!" (The woodchipper's very loud.)
He runs across the snow. Marge can't chase him.

She handcuffs the kidnapper but has to shoot him in the leg,
probably the only time in her career she fires her gun.
In the future, when others run across the snow Marge will chase them.
She muses aloud on greed as she drives. He's silent in the backseat.

"Thelma and Louise" Alternate Ending
for Susan Sarandon and Geena Davis

No driving off the cliff into blue sky.
Instead, you pocket the ignition key,
surrender to a system that will try

you fairly, understanding fully why
you shot a rapist, why you had to flee
and drive off in a panic, warm night sky

embracing, sheltering. You testify,
the courtroom still but steeped in empathy.
Surrender to our system. Wise allies

will counsel you, lend hands and minds, untie
hard knots of fear and guilt, and therapy
will feel like driving into vast blue sky

yet bind you to our earth. Your bright, new life:
belonging to a sisterhood of Me
Too and surrendering the search for why

it happened on your fishing trip. Mourn. Cry.
But hold fast to your ingenuity.
No driving off the cliff into blue sky.
Surrender. Craft new systems. Do not die.

"The Grifters" Sestina
for Anjelica Huston

Lilly Dillon, bleached blonde, tight dress,
high heels at the racetrack, bets big money,
paper clipped in files labelled by race number, answers
to Baltimore bookie Bobo Justus. For longshots
she lowers the odds. She's a cool customer, lies
when she must. At the track in La Jolla, Troubadour

is 70 to 1 in the seventh race. Inside sleek doors
of her Cadillac, Lilly's stuck in gridlock—sleeveless dress
and AC no shield from sweat. Bobo flies
to California when she misses the race, loses money—
big money—for the bookie. Will she be shot,
maimed with a towel full of oranges? The answer,

his lit cigar branding her hand, a milder answer
than we expect, horrible nevertheless behind closed doors.
(Did Huston's contract stipulate the oranges scene would not be
shot?)
Lilly leaves Bobo's hotel with his raincoat over her dress,
admits on occasion she steals a little of his money,
compliments him on his suit, her smile a third lie.

Lilly drops in on her estranged son in "Los Angle-Ease." Roy lies,
says he's a salesman. She doubts this vague answer,
notes clown paintings, black velvet, crummy residential hotel. Money
talk halts abruptly. She dials the phone by the door—
a mob doctor—Roy's belly pain urgent to address.
"My son's gonna be all right." By the ambulance she shoots

a dark glance at the doctor. "If not, I'll have you shot."
Lilly appraises Mrs. Langtry, Roy's "friend". He lies
in the hospital bed, referees two blondes in clingy dresses,
close in age. Venom drips from every question, every answer.
Mrs. Langtry follows Lilly to Phoenix, unlocks the door
of her hotel room to strangle her, steal her money.

Everyone in the whole damn movie pulls cons for money.
Everyone's killed or wounded. With her silencer, Lilly shoots
Mrs. Langtry, swaps clothes and cars, flees to Roy's door,
stuffs cash hidden behind the clowns into a briefcase that lies
on the floor. Roy interrupts. She begs for the money. He answers
coolly, "No." She pivots. Sure, we all pivot. But in Mrs. Langtry's red dress,

Lilly takes one last shot at the money: A long kiss, a new lie—"I'm not
your mother"—then kills him. Briefcase shattering water glass, the final
answer.
He bleeds on the wads. She claws at the cash, closes the door in the stolen
red dress.

"The River Wild" Mirror Sonnet
for Meryl Streep

Gail Hartman, forty something, fit and circumspect—
teacher, mother, wife. Her husband Tom's an architect
too buried in his work to fly to Idaho
for their son Roarke's raft trip. Gail mourns but packs
the gear into the boat, a skilled guide years ago.
Roarke befriends two guys, scores a ball cap from Wade
who chats up Gail, applauds her rafting expertise.
In mid-flirtation, Tom shows up. He's changed his mind.
It turns out Wade and sidekick are ex-cons.
They've pulled a heist. Now on the lam, they need Gail's help.
Wade's got a gun, aims at Roarke's dog. He punches Tom
and kills a cheerful ranger in a red kayak.
Gail and Tom devise a plan: they'll flip the boat, and Wade can't swim.
They reconcile, but Wade won't drown. Gail ends up shooting him.

They reconcile, but Wade won't drown. Gail ends up shooting him.
She and Tom devised the plan to flip the boat. Wade couldn't swim
but killed a cheerful ranger in a red kayak.
Wade had a gun, aimed at Roarke's dog, and punched Tom.
They'd pulled a heist, were on the lam, needed Gail's help.
It turned out Wade and sidekick were ex-cons.
In mid-flirtation Tom showed up. He'd changed his mind
and sought out Gail to praise her rafting expertise but
Roarke befriended two guys, scored a ball cap from Wade.
So much gear in the boat! Gail, a skilled guide years ago,
now led Roarke's raft trip, mourned her husband's pact:
so buried in his work! He flew to Idaho.
Teacher, mother, wife to Tom, an architect—
Gail Hartman, forty something, fit and circumspect.

"Where Angels Fear to Tread" Triolet
for Helen Mirren

Dear Lilia, this time you wed for love—
suave Gino's 21, old world. He cheats,
forbids your walks. He wields an ancient glove.
Dear Lilia, this time you wed for love
but die birthing a brown-eyed son. Your move
to Italy—a vineyard of defeats.
Dear Lilia, you may have wed for love
but Gino's 21, old world. He cheats.

"Dangerous Liaisons" Triolet
for Glenn Close

Silk gowns and powdered wigs—my fine disguise.
I am a virtuoso of deceit.
No one detects the malice in my eyes.
Silk gowns and powdered wigs—my fine disguise
for cruelty. My painted lips purr lies
that lead to dueling on a snowy street.
Silk gowns and powdered wigs—my last disguise.
My epitaph—A Virtuoso of Deceit.

"Rear Window" Pantoum
for Grace Kelly

Lisa Carol Fremont, a fashionista in love with a photojournalist,
flicks on three lamps, one for each of her names, in Jeff's dim apartment.
His leg in a cast, he contemplates breaking up. She's too Park Avenue for him.
She has lobster plus chilled wine delivered from 21, where she lunched earlier.

She flicks on three lamps, one for each of her names. In Jeff's dim apartment,
her playful mood evaporates when he broaches splitting up
after eating lobster plus chilled wine delivered from 21, where she lunched earlier.
She closes the door softly, returns the next night. Another chiffon gown.

Her playful mood evaporates when he broaches splitting up.
She has tenacity and grit, though. She's no lightweight.
Sure, she closes the door softly, returns the next night, another chiffon gown,
but she and the insurance company nurse join forces to solve a crime.

They have tenacity and grit. No lightweights,
they take a shovel, dig for clues. Jeff's stuck watching in his wheelchair.
Lisa and the insurance company nurse join forces to solve a crime.
Jeff's a voyeur, a frozen detective. They're intrepid investigators in high heels.

They take a shovel, dig for clues. Jeff's stuck watching in his wheelchair,
alarmed when Lisa climbs the fire escape into the neighbor Thorwald's window.
The voyeur, frozen detective, watches the intrepid investigator in high heels
and calls the cops, who arrive as Thorwald is just about to strangle her.

Unalarmed, Lisa climbs the fire escape into the neighbor Thorwald's window
looking for more clues, finds the missing wife's wedding ring in a drawer.
The cops arrive as Thorwald is just about to strangle her.
They take her to the precinct for questioning. No handcuffs necessary.

Looking for clues, she'd put on her finger the missing wife's wedding ring.
Off-camera, Lisa brings the cops up to speed: a murder with knives.
At the precinct for questioning, no handcuffs necessary.
But they're essential later: Thorwald breaks in, shoves Jeff out his own window.

Off-camera, Lisa brings the cops up to speed: a murder with knives.
Cops arrive in Jeff's dim apartment, cuff Thorwald who confesses promptly.
What's essential the day after Thorwald breaks in, shoves Jeff out his own window?
A nap. Sunlight on two broken legs. Lisa nearby skimming *Vogue*.

"The Wizard of Oz" Abecedarian
for Clara Blandick

Auntie Em, believe her. While you, Henry and the farmhands huddled
below ground, Dorothy ran with Toto in her arms,
crossed dry Kansas soil, her gingham
dress slapping like a ship's sail. She used
every muscle to pull against the storm cellar door.
Frantic, she stomped again and again with her shoe.
Girls everywhere witnessed the advancing tornado, wished
her family underground would hear her, rescue her. But no,
instead, we saw your house swirl into the sky, Dorothy inside,
journeying alone, so far from her kin. Em, you must be
kind. Be patient with her. Reconciling may take a
long time for you both. She has slept among poppies, seen so
many colors you never will, appraised radical
new ideas, dreaded sand draining through a witch's hourglass.
Oz has changed her.

People do return to their roots, embrace wholeheartedly their
quiet kin, resume crocheting projects, braiding
rugs, canning for winter. Listen closely to her
stories, though, Em. She may speak fondly of scarecrows, lions,
tin men. She may stammer about dark sky
under the wings of flying monkeys, a man's
voice and face enormous in a hall until Toto,
with his small dog mouth, pulled back a curtain
exposing an unremarkable fellow, a huckster in a bolo tie.
Your faith will be tested, Em. Sit together in the parlor, repair
zippers in trousers for the farmhands. There's no place like home.

Appendix: The Movie Makers

Director   **Screenwriter**

Blow (2001)
Ted Demme   David McKenna and Nick Cassavetes
Based on Bruce Porter's 1993 book, *Blow: How a Small Town Boy Made $100 Million with the Medellin Cocaine Cartel and Lost it All*

Dangerous Liaisons (1988)
Stephen Frears   Christopher Hampton
Based on Christopher Hampton's play adapted from Pierre Choderlos de Laclos' 1782 novel

Fargo (1996)
Joel Coen   Joel Coen and Ethan Coen

Fences (2016)
Denzel Washington   August Wilson
Based on August Wilson's 1985 play

Limbo (1999)
John Sayles   John Sayles

Panic Room (2002)
David Fincher   David Koepp

Rear Window (1954)
Alfred Hitchcock   John Michael Hayes

The Grifters (1990)
Stephen Frears   Donald Westlake
Based on Jim Thompson's 1963 novel

The Power of the Dog (2021)
Jane Campion   Jane Campion
Based on Thomas Savage's 1967 novel

The River Wild (1994)
Curtis Hanson   Denis O'Neill

The Walk (2015)
Robert Zemeckis   Robert Zemeckis and Christopher Browne
Based on Philippe Petit's 2002 book *To Reach the Clouds*

The Wings of the Dove (1997)
Iain Softley   Hossein Amini
Based on Henry James' 1902 novel

The Wizard of Oz (1939)
Victor Fleming   Noel Langley, Florence Ryerson, Edgar Allan Woolf
Based on L. Frank Baum's 1900 children's novel

Thelma and Louise (1991)
Ridley Scott   Ridley Scott and Callie Khouri

Titanic (1997)
James Cameron   James Cameron

TransSiberian (2008)
Brad Anderson		Brad Anderson and Will Conroy

Where Angels Fear to Tread (1991)
Charles Sturridge		Tim Sullivan, Derek Granger, Charles Sturridge
Based on the 1905 novel by E.M. Forster

Wind River (2017)
Taylor Sheridan		Taylor Sheridan

In Appreciation

So many creative souls inspired and supported the making of this book. Special thanks to Jan Beatty, Rebecca Foust, and Lynne Thompson. I've admired Nancy Buffum's artistry for over thirty years; I'm delighted that her bracing, brilliant work graces this book cover as well as the covers of *Almost the Rowboat* and *A Juror Must Fold in on Herself.* I'm grateful to my students and colleagues at Skyline College and OLLI-San Francisco, astute writer friends in two long-running Bay Area poetry groups, and members of my San Francisco poetry master class, especially Elise Kazanjian who hosts us so warmly in her gorgeous home on the 17th floor. Thank you, too, fellow Unitarian Universalists and MacGuffinistas and all the kind strangers I passed on sidewalks during COVID. I feel grateful for my widening and deepening circle of family and friends. There are way too many beloveds to name here! You know who you are. Most of all, love and cuddles to Tom and Inky.

Kathleen McClung is the author of five poetry collections: *Questions of Buoyancy, A Juror Must Fold in on Herself*, winner of the 2020 Rattle Chapbook Prize, *Temporary Kin, The Typists Play Monopoly* and *Almost the Rowboat*. She co-authored with Mary Kennedy Eastham and Eileen Malone *Three Soul-Makers: Poems That Bring Us Together*. Winner of the Morton Marr, Maria W. Faust, and Rita Dove national poetry prizes, her work appears in a variety of journals and anthologies. A 2024 finalist for San Francisco Poet Laureate, she served from 2021-23 as guest editor for *The MacGuffin*, a print literary journal based in Michigan. She also served as associate director of the Soul-Making Keats literary competition and judged the contest's sonnet category. In 2018-2019 she was a writer-in-residence at Friends of the San Francisco Public Library. Kathleen teaches literature and writing classes at Skyline College in San Bruno and directed the Women on Writing conference there for ten years. She also teaches privately and at Osher Lifelong Learning Institute (OLLI) in San Francisco. Visit her website at *www.kathleenmcclung.com*

www.ingramcontent.com/pod-product-compliance
Lightning Source LLC
Chambersburg PA
CBHW022058080426
42734CB00009B/1406